Life Is the Journey

Saying Goodbye to 2020 & 2021

by David W. Markkula

DORRANCE
PUBLISHING CO
EST. 1920
PITTSBURGH, PENNSYLVANIA 15238

Dorrance Publishing Co
585 Alpha Drive
Suite 103
Pittsburgh, PA 15238
Visit our website at *www.dorrancebookstore.com*

ISBN: 978-1-6853-7406-8
eISBN: 978-1-6853-7550-8

Life is the Journey

Life is the journey

The choices we make are chances we take

There are no mistakes, just lessons we learn

Let's take a chance on each other and discover

life together Finding you was fate and a blessing

I'll take a chance on the future, as it's not set,

but what we make of it

Take a chance with me I wont let you down

Let's take this journey together and

dance in the rain

Sharing this journey with you can only be

what life should be

Let's take a chance and shoot for the stars

The life that will be will have a few bumps here

and there but beautiful just the same, and

wonderful to share

Lives that Inspired Me

This book is dedicated to the people who's lives inspired me throughout my life.

I can only hope that I can make there souls live in my words.

For those I've lost in this last year by death or by my own

Stupidity of forgetting who I was and who I want to be. As I write these words, I hope that I find myself again, to heal the world that came crashing down around us. I hope that I can now feed a soul by giving you a little of mine and leaving a little piece of my heart in yours. I hope that those I write about dance with you one more time and that their story touches you.

You Were the Spark

You were the spark that started it all and didn't know it

I didn't know it myself until it was to late

You gave me love and life while I gave you grief but loved

you just the same

You taught me much more than you know; it just took me a lifetime to realize it myself

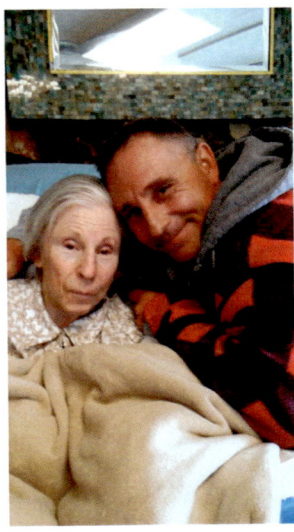

Mom in her early 20s and just before her death

in May of 2017, at 75 years young.

My mom had what most consider to be selfless
life, but when I think about it I consider it to be
extraordinary. She cared more about others and
serving them. She was a nurse and cared for so
many most of her life. Which is something pretty
amazing. So when she was diagnosed with
Alzheimer's it was hard on everyone because it
was she that needed the care she had once given.
I was there every weekend to sit with her. My
only regret is that for the first few years that's all
I did. It wasn't until her final year I started
remembering her and the wonderful things she
did throughout her lifetime. That's when I started
writing about the little things that no one ever
thinks about. I would sit and write and read them
to her and the smile she had would just light up.
Nurses would come by and say they never see

her smile so much. Now a few things I wrote for Mom while we remembered together.

Treasured Time

A mother holds her baby at birth for the first time

Exhausted yet smiling and happy with

tears of joy

Filled with joy as she and baby are tickling,

giggling, cooing and wooing

From the first steps and first words, the

wonders grow

As we play and grow, scrapes and cuts will

happen, and mom is there to comfort us with

hugs and kisses as she puts a band-aid on

Mom is there as we grow older through good

times and bad times, sharing our joys and pains

of a first love and lost

She's been there before and knows

just what to say

Mom's there when we bring our little one into
the world and helps whenever she can
Mom's curse is a blessing
"I hope your children are just like you"
As mom was there at the beginning throughout
my life, I remember her treasured moments and
they become my Treasured Time
4/20/17

A Quilt in Time

You gathered each piece of fabric
Each piece a memory in time
You sewed them together one by one, connecting
them all with a fabric of love
Each quilt telling a story for who you
sewed it for
Each story special for who you gave it to
It matters not who has the last one, but to have
one of my own is special for me

Its story will be remembered by all, as it is

passed from generation to generation, with the

love that you sewed

April 2017

Mom loved to make and create things. From ceramic crafts to Christmas ornaments or just anything she found. She would create to give gifts to last a lifetime.

Baking with Mom

There was a time when we would bake cookies
together

I would help mix at first

Each time I would do a little more

I didn't know but you were teaching me
something

We moved on to cooking with much more to do
on holidays All the wonderful flavors that came

Your lessons were given with love

The comfort you gave with each dish that we
made was a blessing to have

I cook alone now, but will always remember that
time with you

Some things will never be as good as mom made
but I know I wont starve because she taught me

how to fend for myself when I'm hungry.
Sometimes if you want something you just have
to make it yourself.

Life

Life comes and goes

Life is now

Life is learning from the past and moving
forward

Life's most precious moment is now

Don't dwell on the past, for you lose focus on the
future

Life is simply living in the moment

Life is now

Life is you and lives in your heart
and soul

Nurses

the Forgotten Heroes

We see them every day

They think not of themselves but only of others

They care for us every day when we can't for
ourselves

They give us our dignity back so we can have
peace of mind, body and soul

Nurses are the forgotten heros, always caring
and loving, giving all they have to share

Their hearts always full, with plenty of joy and a
smile to brighten the day

As I said, my mom was a nurse for many years and worked for the VA convalescent care. My niece followed in her footsteps because of my mom, her grandmother. She doesn't hear it enough from me, but I'm proud of her and the service she gives to those under her care.

Clouds

Clouds float across a bright blue sky,

forever changing, always moving,

opening new paths to follow and never ending

Life is clouds floating across the sky, a journey

to be embraced and never ending

Mom

God's Gift

Moms are angels

They look after their children with precious,

caring, tender love, always guiding

and protecting

We may not always like the answers that they

give us as children

But the answers given were pure and for our

well being

Mom's lessons throughout our lives are God's

gift of strength and love to us all

I thank God Mom is my Angel

A New Angel

I think of Mom and how much she meant to everyone she touched

The love that she gave to so many through her kind heart and caring soul

I think of her now as one of God's Guardian Angels

When I hear the bells toll, I'll know she'll have her wings

She'll smile, keeping watch over us, protecting us as we journey through life

I wasn't able to get there in time to say goodbye to my mom that day. I had a friend who gave me the peace of mind and comfort to be able to write that and let out what I was feeling. To my friend I can't thank you enough. I can't tell you how much you meant to me that day and the ones following. Thank you my dear friend.

I'd like to share with you a poem I wrote for my shining light. While I haven't thought it was completely finished maybe we can all add our own verse as we remember our shining light.

Every Day Shines
Every day shines in a different light
Whether it's sunny or dark and rainy
Every day shines in a different light

The sun shines and warms our hearts to new heights

Every day shines in a different light
The darkest rainy day brings us fresh new air,
rejuvenating new life
Every day shines in a different light
A cold winter's snow so crisp and light,
we make snow angels dance
Every day shines in a different light
Mom made every day shine

About one month before her passing is when I wrote this one. I was thinking back to my childhood past. It was my sixth birthday, on a Mother's Day. My shining light baked a cake. The cake said "Happy Birthday David" and "Happy Mother's Day". I was selfish and didn't understand. Now a 6 year old child doesn't understand the significance of sharing the cake. I certainly didn't. I thought it was MY day, MY cake. My mom could see I was disappointed. The next day she made another cake while I was at school. It was German chocolate - my favorite, as long as it's made by Mom. I shared it with her and only with her. Dad wanted some but he understood what was up. That's just one of the countless things Mom would do to see that her children were happy.

Thirty years later, my godson was born on my Mother's Day, same day as myself. I told my best friend this story and he said make sure you never have just one cake on that day. The first time his birthday fell on Mother's Day they had two cakes. To top it off his parents hired a retired fireman, who had a vintage firetruck, and he gave all the kids a ride on top of it. It was kinda like the were in their own parade through the neighborhood.

As I grew older, we grew apart by time and distance. But she was still my shining light. While I was in the service, in my travels I saw a nutcracker and thought of my shining light. So I sent my Shining Light the nutcracker as a Christmas gift. She cherished it and never put it away, keeping it out year round, for all to enjoy. She gave it her own personal touch, adorning it, making it special to her. Every Christmas she would send me my stocking filled with goodies, to keep my spirits up. She did it for all her children, spreading her joy. As I returned home from the service, it was her time to travel the world. But she was still always there for us all. In these final years, as I sat with her, I remembered what made her my Shining Light. To my brothers and sister - we all have our own stories of what makes our Shining Light. All of them special to each of us, in every day and in every way. While we mourn the loss of our mom, let us also celebrate her life by remembering her for the shining light that she is.

Your Journey Continues

Remembering you Mom and all the love you gave us throughout your life

We mourn your loss, but celebrate your life as well

Your presence here on earth was a gift from God

You touched so many lives in so many ways with a gentle touch and warm, caring heart

Always giving when you could, even when it was hard, never asking for anything in return

Your journey continues with us as you will always be in our hearts and never more than a thought of you away

Your journey continues with God now; as he holds you close in his arms, you continue to watch over us from high above Your journey with us here may have ended, but your journey in Heaven is just beginning

You're one of God's angels now, our Guardian Angel

The destination is the journey and there is no end

Dad

I look across the deep blue sea on a cool

winter's day

As I cast your ashes to the winds of time I see a

falcon fly across the sky and know your

soul is free

Looking down on us as we remember you

I guess you could say my dad inspired me in a different way. I think maybe that is where I get the dreamer in me from. Dad was a pilot but not the commercial kind. He flew just for fun, as a hobby. I can only remember going up one time with him alone, when I was about 5. My older brother went with him several times. We both loved going fishing with him. There was always a story or two. I got to believe them too, because I've seen him catch some big fish. There were not just fishing stories, but stories of his hunting and his travels. He would take the family to Tahoe on a spur of the moment and just live the dream and take it as it comes.

For a long time, I felt bad or guilty when he passed away, because for about two weeks before his passing he tried to call and talk with me every day. I just didn't talk or answer the phone because it was always the same conversation. So maybe I was being selfish by not wanting to talk with him. When my aunt called to say he was in the hospital for a failing liver it was like I got hit in the head with a bat. The next day she called from the hospital and they put the phone to his ear so that I could say hi, and that I love him. He passed shortly after, about 15 minutes later. I still felt guilty though. Until a few months later when my brothers and sister went to the coast to cast his ashes into the ocean, where he wanted to be.

As I cast his ashes, I turned around and a huge rogue wave came out of nowhere and just engulfed me. I was soaked head to toe. It was like my dad was saying one last time "I got ya kid". That's when I came to my peace with how I felt about my dad.

Is it Really Fall

Is it really Fall? What happened to Spring?
The rejuvenation of life, the awakening and
rebirth of what's to come
Or Summer, where did it go? How did I miss the
flourishing growth and beauty in the world?

The end of summer has left me feeling crushed and defeated

I feel I've lost so much and lost sight of who I am and who I want to be

Part of me welcomes change, but not change to forget the past and lost time

Change to grow and move forward, but not alone

Change together and accept what we feel

But with a space to grow

Fall is here and we've lost so much this year; it feels like winter never really ended

I ache for this winter to end and the return of spring to rejuvenate my soul so that it may once again flourish in summer

This is the change I welcome; my hope is we can make it through and grow

Together we're stronger, and even in the dead of winter, new life can be found that will heal our souls, to thrive with a love for life.

That's how I felt in October of 2020 when I thought things couldn't get any worse for me. At that point I had lost one of the best friends I ever had. Losing that friend was because I lost myself and tried to help too much, when all I had to do was just be there and be supportive. There were a few others also because of the politicization of Covid19. I don't feel so bad about those ones now because if a few differences can't be set aside then they really weren't the friends I needed anyway. December came and it all crashed down on my family even harder. My niece and nephew had tested positive for Covid19 on Christmas Day. Then a few days later, my sister and brother in law. My sister took about a month to recover but her husband never did. He passed on January 29. 2021. My heart wept for my sister and her kids. I even started to cry myself. I wrote this when I heard the news.

My Brother Glenn

A brother whose time ended all too soon

I look back and remember you

The memories are countless, and in them time stands still for you

Your soul will live in our hearts now

I'll miss all the little things you did for me

Most of all I'll miss the many years of happiness you gave my sister

Rest In Peace now my brother and know you are and will always be loved

End of Life and DNR

End of life and how one can ask another to simply unplug. I look back and remember the day the doctors gathered my brothers and sister to talk about our mom and prepare us for the inevitable. Mom was with us another 4 1/2 years. So in this uncertain time of Covid19, I ask that of myself again and think of what my little sister is going through now, as her children are with her going through this again. The pain she feels and I cannot be there for her. She knows she has my thoughts and prayers. She knows that her husband, my other brother, have my thoughts and prayers, hoping for him to pull through and that this decision to unplug doesn't come. How does one honor the wishes of a DNR or go against it? I'm torn apart by this now, as I have always thought that if I could not breathe on my own to just let me go. There are many things in life right now that are tearing me apart that I cannot control. In it all I try to find myself and answers that will heal.

Believing

It started with my grandpa. Long ago, shortly after I was born, my grandpa had just finished his ministry school and was newly ordained. I was his first baptism I'm told. I grew up going to church every Sunday. I sang in the church choir, even had a few solos here and there. I had a leading role in Shadrach, Meshach and Abednego. I played Abednego. There was Bible study too. In my teens I attended confirmation classes once or twice a week. How Grandpa would have loved to be there for that. When I was older, I went off to serve in the Army. Although I stopped going to church, I still Believed. In time I met a woman, got married and divorced in the same year. I felt as though the weight of the world had come down on me with a vengeance. I questioned my Faith and struggled with it. I knew I needed to talk to someone, so I turned to Grandpa, the only person of faith I would want to speak with at the time. It was hard because I knew it would break his heart. He told me that it's going to be alright. That god is watching and that his plan isn't always clear, that there are struggles and triumphs. He told me I don't have to go to church to believe. That all I need is the ground I stand on, whether it's high on a mountain top, on a park bench, or even a coat closet in the dark. It doesn't matter where I pray. He was happy I came to him with my loss of faith. He helped me regain that faith and restore what was. I don't thump my Bible at others, but I Believe and that's all that matters.

A Soul Cries

A soul cries and its cry is silent but heard

Its pain is felt by the love that surrounds it

Through space and time it will heal

It's the hug and kiss of another soul that brings

comfort from the heart

A smile opens the door

I wrote this for a friend originally at a time when she was feeling down and alone. She shut herself out of the world to shelter. I found myself reading this often during the last 18 months and started thinking this is for me too, as my soul was crying also. Now it's for everyone who needs to know they aren't alone in the world. There is always someone there for you. This next part was added as I was putting this book together.

A Soul

When the door opens, the smile you see was

always there for you

Don't be afraid of what it may bring

Embrace the moment

For the life in it is meant for you

It's encouragement and love that we feel that will

heal a crying soul

A Time for Strength

There is I time for everything. A time where
everything seems to come down all around us
and has the weight of the world on our
shoulders. It's times like this that makes us
stronger with every second. During these times
we find our will to endure and that is our gift to
each other. The strength we give each other
brings us closer and flourishes into something
far greater than what we had imagined. I see that

strength in you by the spark in your eyes. I see it by the beautiful smile you have. I hear it in your sweet voice. I feel it with your soft touch and every heartbeat we share. Our story has always been and will always be in our souls as we find a strength in our hearts giving to each other what has always been.

Smile for me, as today is a better day

These two were written for a very good friend that was sad for many reasons, but I feel that they hold true for everyone now.

2020 was a year that we all wish didn't happen and that we could just forget. I found myself losing faith in God and lost a brother and one of the best friends I ever had. There's nothing I can do about one but to give my support to the family. The other all I can do is hope the time will heal and that one day that friend will return. I pray every night for the safety and well-being of everyone I know.

The Path I Choose

The path I choose, it is who I aspire to be that defines me

In every step I take you're always in my heart and with me every step along the way

With every step I take a new adventure takes shape

Hold my hand let's take a walk together with open hearts

Where we go is up to you; as long as we're together is all that matters

The path I choose is with you

My soul always with you and found in the heart even when we're apart

In some way I could be talking to myself as I feel like my soul is at time not with me and going the same direction as my body. Sometimes I just don't know.

Wine and Dine in Turbulent Times

We made the time to wine and dine in the these

turbulent times

We went shopping and found your brand, then some yard stones for the garden and had more

than a few laughs along the way

In between, a place with spirits that remembered

a time of prohibition and a guy named Hooker

who had a thing for courtesan ladies

A century agave spikes ready to yield the world's

finest tequila for two masked friends to partake

A stroll through the gardens and another bottle

of wine in a shaded spot to keep cool from the

afternoon heat

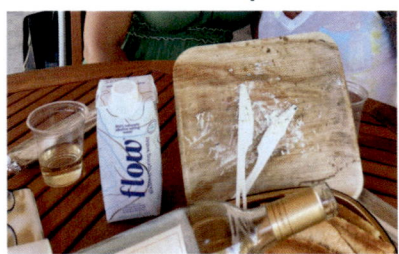

A sphere captured your eyes nestled away under the trees with a bench just for you to sit and take refuge for just a little bit

I sucked down olives and made them pop as they went in to make you all laugh

Just friends taking time for each other to get the other through this turbulent time of c19

In my heart I know this one is unfinished as I was unable to find out what the fondest memory of that day was from each of them. I leave the three of you all a blank page to finish it for yourself, and the hope that one day you can share it with me. To everyone else, if it applies to you, by all means give it true meaning to yourselves as well and use the blank page.

Separate Journeys, Adventures Shared

Each journey is our own and never ending
Adventures shared with the other is the life and
heartbeat of the other
The adventures we shared will always be
remembered and
cherished in the others journey

So many things have been shared through the years. Most of them are beautiful things and places done. Living for the moment will be with me forever. I know that they all hold a special place in the hearts and memories of those I shared them with. One day we'll reminisce together and laugh at the great times or cry at how it all ended.

You Did it America

You were asked to do things that were unselfish. You wore a mask and kept your distance to slow the spread. You did it and then they changed what the goal was and asked for more. Closing everything that is essential. Not just convenient but essential; things like dentists, chiropractic health care, parks and recreational activities outside that are vital to a healthy body. Things that are essential to healthy body and socially distanced by nature. You were unselfish America. You did it, and then they STOPPED asking and TOLD you to give more. They stepped over a line. They threatened to fine and jail law abiding citizens while releasing criminals. But you continue to do it because you are unselfish. They have looked away at those who are selfish and do things to destroy private businesses and disrupt our lives while telling us we have to give more or we're the selfish ones. All while they don't practice what they the preach. They tell you all this knowing you did it America, you slowed the spread and that was unselfish and all you could do. The spread will happen regardless and herd immunity, with a vaccine, together will crush this. Keeping the economy closed will do nothing but hurt. Telling people not to be people, and stay apart and divided, will only prolong the disruption in our lives. It's not staggeringly

selfish of us to want back what we gave up.
America you were unselfish and it's time that
what you gave up be given back. If they won't
open up and give it back we need to take it back.

Here we are over a year later. At every step of progress we make, there are those in some states and the federal and some state governments that want to keep changing the goal and threshold to keep a temporary power. The time is beginning to near though and its actually beginning to feel like the spring we all lost. Things beginning to open again. Sitting inside at restaurant or in the winery. Depending on the state you're in. you can enter a building without a mask. How relieving is that going to be for banks? LOL, I mean up until now only a masked bank robber did that.

You Can Kneel as I Still Stand

You can take a knee to take your stand

Just remember that it was I and millions more

who will always stand so that you can

take your knee

We all stand in one way or another for what we

believe; it has nothing to do with race,

religion or gender

I'll continue to stand so that you can

take your knee

Just respect me and others like me and remember

we stood for you, regardless of what you

think of us

I'll always stand for what I believe

The Dirty Dozen

We are the dirty dozen with a silent digital death. Though it was silent it had a huge roar. Brothers forever to the end we will be. We may not know each other very well anymore but we will always know what others can never understand about brothers like us. I think of you all from time to time and hope you're all doing well.

A Patch of Grass

It was a patch of grass that brought a touch of

home and lifted spirits to my brothers, in a land

far from home

I captured it and placed a sign upon it

Stay off the grass

We kept it with us and took it

everywhere we went

The water given with a newfound love of life

We trimmed it with a pair of scissors for a time

This patch gave us all a comfort of home in a

place far from home

This patch of grass brought with it a sense of home to me. I'm sure it brought the same to my Brothers. I know at the very least it made them laugh. I don't remember who did it, but one of them put that patch of grass in a mess kit pan and we took it with us everywhere for a while. That's a memory that has stayed with me for over 30 years now. I think of it often and know I made a difference at a time of stress and brought a smile to the hearts of my Brothers. My brother Rudy sent that picture to me after we had a 30-year reunion. It made me realize that some things will ALWAYS be. It gave me hope that ALWAYS exists and will ALWAYS be.

Stars and Stripes

Stars and Stripes wave for all to see

Our brave defend her for all to rejoice in

Some walk a thin blue line

Only if all could remember the brave

who give so much

13 Folds

13 folds that always touch my soul and have a

place in my heart

If you have one you know how I feel

WE HONOR THEM BECAUSE THEY

HONORED ALL

I don't talk about my days in the Army very often other than I had served. Not because I don't want to, but because most people wouldn't understand or appreciate what I would be saying. This spring of 2021 I will be with my Brothers in Arms, the brothers I went to Desert Storm with. We've all been talking and planning, in group text it's funny how many things we all remember, and its been 30 years. To be able to see and talk will just be incredible and healing for the heart and soul this spring.

A Silent Abyss

Silence, the deepest darkest realm of hell

No comfort can be found there

Silence is the abyss, a living hell

There is no escape for the hell is in the mind,

It tears away at the soul and crushes the heart

The abyss, silent and cold, a living hell

I was feeling down when I wrote that. It was just how I felt. Due to Covid19, I found myself and many others feeling that again, through all the lockdowns. I know I'm not alone in that feeling and that together we can change or heal what was lost in the chaos.

Fear

The things we fear the most are the unknown

Lay them to rest and embrace the future

Take the lessons learned and

change what you can

Family and friends are always there for love and support Fear will be no more

I'm always here with you

Let's all face our fears and crush them. It is our fear that keeps us from living.

Tomorrow Never Comes

Tomorrow never comes without a little hope and
a dream
Stay true to yourself and tomorrow will come

The time is always now. What you do with it is what matters most. The time is now. It's your time to live.

Wondering Star

I often look at the stars and when I look at yours
I no longer see the twinkle in it that I once saw
I wonder to myself and think of what
could have been
I imagine looking into your eyes to see the spark
that once lit your star

Then I can't help but think "can the feelings once shared be rekindled into lighting your star again"
I want to reach out and send you a message but can't seem to find the strength

Someday I'll have the courage and reach for you. In the last year I've faced my greatest fear and lost the best friend I ever had. We knew each other so well. She knew me better than anyone ever has and understood me. If I could change time I would, but I can't. There is nothing else I could lose in life that could take me down. So I hold on to my hopes and dreams with faith in God that there is a reason for all that's happened. I'm not letting go. It's just not who I am. Something inside me tells me it's not the end and what that means I don't know. But it's something that I will keep my heart open to exploring, when the time comes.

There Was a Time

There was a time that there was nothing that came between us. Our thoughts were one, as if we were together from the very start. Only separated by time. The space was never too great to overcome. As in every journey there are ripples in the seabed that cause a tidal wave. Lost in a storm I look to the stars to find you again. So that we may learn to dance once more. The storm may be strong but no storm is stronger than the souls and hearts of two friends that have always been in the heart. Like an angel, you are always with me in my heart. It's OK to let me in yours. I know it's complicated. You know what's in my heart. You know how I feel. You know I'm here for you and that you have my support in everything you do. If I could change the things I can't control, I would. It's not up to me. I wish it was. It's OK to let me in your heart. Together we can change the things we want to change when the time is right for us. If I make you smile, I mean to. Because there's something there. If I make you feel special, I mean to. Because there's something there. It's OK to let me in your heart. If I make you laugh, I want to. Because there is something there. It's OK to let me in your heart. You're in mine. Tell me how you feel. I won't let you down. Will you take a chance with me? There's nothing wrong. Only what's right for us. It's OK to share our hearts.

We've been through so much and I know in my heart that there is something there. What that means exactly I don't know, but its something I'll take a chance on and just let it grow one day at a time.

A Ripple in My Heart

You're the ripple that flows through my heart and feeds my soul

I wait for the day to hold you again

I'd like to think I made a ripple too

We are but a drop in the sea, but the ripple we make is everlasting and felt for all time

*To have walked with you on the beach and
venture into the sea was more than I could have
ever wanted
The time shared is the ripple that flows in my
heart*

See the Dream and Live the Dream
*Close your eyes and imagine
Open your mind, your soul; let go and
see the dream unfold
As you feel the dream grow in your heart, open
it up and fan the flames of desire
The passion inside you will awaken as you
begin to dream
I live the dream every day
I feel the dream unfold before my very eyes
This dream, this journey of life
My dream is never ending as I live
Be the dream catcher and live your dreams*

A friend once told me that "you're living in a dream world". I wanted to tell that friend they live in the same dream world I do. For reasons I wont get into here. it's best to just let that go. I will say, as much as it hurt at the time, I did not want to return the hurt. That said, it made me think of self-forgiveness and that's when I wrote these next ones.

One Day
One day I'll forgive myself for what I became

All I ever wanted to do was make a difference

In doing so, I lost who I was and became a monster I could not see

Because I did not listen, I lost who and what was most important in my life

One day I'll forgive myself and pray you have forgiven me too

One day you'll forgive yourself and know just
how beautiful you truly are
Your heart will open and you'll see what has
always been inside of you
You'll feel what has always been with you....

When I began writing those, I was remembering my mom and little brother also. When I was 18 and living in Germany, my little brother had been abused by our mom's second husband. For many years after that she carried with her a guilt that was never talked about. I didn't know about it myself until more recent years, but I knew that for the better part of 20 years that something had happen because mom went out of her way to make sure my little brother was taken care of whenever he needed anything. Whether she had forgiven herself or my brother told her that he's OK, that she did the best she could, that there's nothing to be forgiven for, I don't know. I'd like to think it was the latter, but either way an inner peace was found between the two of them. It wasn't until then that my mom remarried, for the third time, to someone she had been with for 20 years. That's the short story. I know for many it has relevance and I say to you "You have nothing to be forgiven for. You did your best and you gave all you could, doing was you felt was right, You have nothing to feel guilty for". I know that sometimes we all need to hear it from the other person involved. I know I could certainly use that, but for now I get up every day and tell myself that I need to forgive myself. Some days are better than others.

We've all done things in our lives that we may not be proud of or happy with how we acted. The first step in fixing or righting what was wrong is starting with ourselves and asking for forgiveness. Some day, and I look forward to that day, I'll have both. That's my hope. My hope is that you find inner peace as well.

Now you have a brief insight to who I am or at least to how I feel about life and a few people who have greatly influenced me and affected me. I invite you into my world of dreams fantasy and reality. Enjoy the stars, beaches, and places I've seen and been. Walk with me now.

My Star
My Star belongs to you
It will forever shine bright because of you
It has always been your beautiful smile that
made me shine

Night Falls

Night falls and stars rise like the sea our souls live and love Bright is the night filled with souls of stars

I only see your star; in your star dreams are real as the soul lives and loves

As a shooting star is wished upon, so is each wave that shapes the beach as the souls that find peace in the night

As a new day dawns your soul is a siren of the sea like your star in the night

Ride your wave across the sea and find your beach to live and love, as your dream is real

Sharing a piece of this with you is the life we

live and love

Open Hearts

It is the open heart that soars as it is free

Our hearts are open with an exhilarating

passion to explore

An open heart is tender and caring and

felt by another

Our hearts are healing with a power that

feeds the soul

It is the soul that flows through the heart

We are open hearts

A Sea of Ecstasy

A siren calls to me and I find myself at lands'

end, in silky golden sands, at a sea of ecstasy

A fire begins to stir within, and I enter the warm

waters of the sea, in search of the siren that

calls to me

Drawn to the deep blue, my siren appears

Enchanted by her beauty, a new journey begins

Sun Rise

As the sun rises, it kisses us and we

glisten and shine

With the warmth, a passion of life with fire in

our hearts will rise

Let's take time to enjoy the suns rise and the day

it brings us

An Inspiring Beach

I stroll down the beach on a warm summer day,

leaving behind me what was

As every new wave crosses my feet

a beautiful new path awaits my soul to bless

Sharing that with you

is all I want out of Life

Memories Kept

Driftwood that caught the eyes and shaped
just right

Seashells of different types; some glitter with
shiny surface, others with nothing more than just
an odd shape

Sand dollars; some big, some small, some
perfectly rounded and others rough

It is the memories in the things saved that I
cherish the most

For those memories are special to more than
just one

It is in the objects collected that we see those
memories that clearly are special and know
they're in our hearts

and still found in the things that are kept

I can feel our toes buried in the sand

My Best Friend

My best friend is someone who inspires me

She knows what I'm thinking and can finish my

thoughts, and I hers

I see how beautiful she is, not just with my eyes

but with my heart

The smile we see in each other is the smile we

see in our souls and feel in our hearts

She is kind, caring and loving

The warmth in her soul is felt through her heart

and seen in her beautiful smile

I know her as she knows me

You/she are my best friend

The First Dance

The first dance we shared she wore a blue dress

and high heels

The music was soft and slow, we felt the passion

in each other

With a kiss, a desire was released like a storm

with a heartbeat that would not be stopped

What came next is only for you and me to know

This dance is not done, for time stands still…

Chasing the Bear

Sitting on the deck having an afternoon drink, I heard a shout. "BEAR". I got up and came around front and we all saw a bear running down the street. How cool was this to see. We gave chase. As we got to the end of the street, there he was standing at the house on the corner, peeping in windows, going from one to the next. He looked at us and ran off across the street into the forest, between other cabins. We gave chase. Again. He stopped at another, looked back and roamed around for a bit. Off he went again. And we gave chase. Again. He stopped in the street to look back at us. I walked up to get a closer snapshot, heart pounding with excitement. I had never seen a bear in the wild before. I got within 50 feet. Maybe closer, I don't know. I can tell you it was close enough.

He was a big bear. In one leap he was up and out of the street, up the hill and back into the forest. Never to be seen again. Looking back, I would give chase again.

Live life and Chase the Bear with me.

North Star

There is but one star of the night

that's always true and bright

The North Star always bright, always

guiding those that are lost

Never wavering, always true to its light

You're the Star of my life

by day or night

My Soul

My Soul is free

My Soul belongs to me and me alone

My Soul is mine to share with who I want to

share it with

My Soul is not yours to take or keep

My Soul is free

Your soul is free

Your soul belongs to you and you alone

Your soul is yours to share with whom you want

I don't want to take your soul

I only want to share a piece of mine with yours

You have my soul; you have always had my soul

and I choose to share it with you and you alone

A Perfect Storm

A storm approaches and I smell the rain

It excites and awakens the soul

I feel the rain and a tingling sensation cleanses

my soul Lightning strikes and ignites a fire

Its raw power is felt in the heart

The thunder rolls and that power is released

With it a passion that can't be stopped

You're my perfect storm and have captured my soul, my heart, and it calms me to know you are the life in the storm

Let us dance together now

Though you are my perfect storm, you are the harmony within my heart that gave me peace and the patience to dance in the rain.

A Rising Star

As I watch the sunrise, the dawn of a new day begins

The promise of a bright new day is on the rise as it begins to blaze across the sky, giving a warm feeling that refreshes the soul

When I close my eyes and take it in, I feel it in me and see another star on the rise

The star I see is you

The trail you blaze is in the heart and the warmth felt is tenfold over the one in the sky

I feel a sensation come over me

My soul is filled with the promise of a glorious and beautiful day

You're felt my the heart and it is a sea of wonderful and amazing things to be discovered

This journey of a new day with you is the rising star

A Kiss

A kiss can be soft and gentle

Warm and tender

Deep and passionate

Moist and wet

Closed lip to opened lip with tongues

swirling around

Imagine our kiss

Wonderful, mild and wild, with much greater

things to come

Let's share an amazing kiss together

The journey will be incredible

To have had your kiss will always be with me in my heart and in my soul. When I wrote that I was trying to imagine the perfect kiss. Now I believe the perfect kiss is always what's felt and shared between two people.

Butterfly

You are the butterfly that has weathered the

storms and trials of the past

You've triumphed over them and

learned to dance

You're strong at heart, yet soft and delicate

As you spread your wings and take flight with

the grace and elegance of an angel dancing

among the clouds, you

catch my eyes, you touch my heart and bless my

soul with your true beauty

True Beauty

Your true beauty is in your soul

Your true beauty can be found in your heart

Your true beauty is seen in your bright eyes and

your amazing smile

Your true beauty is felt with an open heart

Your true beauty is who you are

Rain on Me

Rain on me and I'll show you how

beautiful your smile is

Rain on me and I'll show you a

rejuvenating dance

Rain on me and I'll give you a feeling

beyond extraordinary

Rain on me and together we'll dance to

a new day

A Sea Full of Life

You're the sea that's full of life

You're the life that's in the sea

You're the soul in the sea that is the

beauty with in it

You're the siren of the sea and like an angel, you

watch over her

You're the sea that lives in the heart

On the edge of the sea, as you walk on

golden beaches,

calm waves wash away the past

and every step you take is new

You're the sea in my heart that I treasure always

The Futures

A night at the futures with you

Tasting what was to be

We lift our glasses to taste what would be

From one barrel to the next, another

flavor to savor

The sunshine that was captured in the bottle now set in us These grapes, these delicious grapes, now releasing the sunshine back to us

The Sea Called

The sea called and I answered

As I stepped onto a golden beach that she shaped
with her gentle yet powerful waves of wonder
and beauty, I

saw before me a mermaid angel of the sea, that
kept watch over Her and those that dare to enter
into Her

She welcomed me with an open heart and the
most

amazing smile that captured my soul

As we played in the shallows of the cove, a fire
began to stir and I was given a trident spear

As I was given the power to explore and
discover the treasure within Her heart and soul,
our desires and passions were released

Ode to Silver

An honest man takes to an open road
as if in flight
Destinations unknown as he searches for that

to which he commits

Along the way he takes rest and gathers at

a watering hole

He sits and tells his story and others stand in

awe, wishing that they could be the

legend before them

He takes another bite and chases it down with

another ale, and a new tale begins

Thinking to myself I say, "I hope he finds it", as

I seek to find the same

Although we take a different path to find the one

It's the adventure to get there that's

the envy of others

I'm just a fellow patron with a

journey of my own

Just remember the journey is the destination, that

there is no end and everything else is a series of

adventures that are who we are

Reach Out

Reach out to touch the Heart

The Soul you find will open to you
The warm glow from within will flow into yours

Once Open and Warm Now Cold

A heart once open and warm filled with
hopes and dreams
A heart that found another to give everything
it had
Now cold and empty; trying to hold on to hope
so that one day it can dream again and live
All it needs is to feel what it lost, to open once
more and dream
What was lost was real and will always
be in the heart and in the soul

What was lost can be found again, as it will

always be

I believe everything can be renewed, that some

things are worth it

In the end it will make us stronger

No Room For Hate

I have no room in my heart for hate

Where there is sorrow and sadness I find hope

knowing there is a time and place for everything

In my memories will always be the things that

were special

I try to learn from my mistakes and can only ask

for forgiveness

Anger is only temporary and will in time subside

Until then I will wish you all the best and keep

you in my heart

An Open Mind

To my friends I am an open mind
They see me for who I am
They see me for who I want to be
They see who I am in my heart
I am who I am because of them
I am who I am because of my best friend
You bring out the best in me

There are things in life that are sometimes said that are not meant. That was something I was thinking about when this was written. Some of the things I've written were written in frustration, anger, hope, how I would like to see the world, dreams or fantasy. I feel it's important to say this because regardless of what has happened, I never felt hate.

World Without Colors

I see a world of colors all bright and unique

Each color brings out the beauty in the other

No one color stands without the other

To say any one color matters more than the other

is blind to the vibrancy of the world

Imagine a sunrise and see the

beauty in the world

Now imagine it without all the colors

What was bright and beautiful,

now dull without life

It takes all colors to make one stand out more
than the others
Each will have its spotlight in its own time
It's in our eyes that we see a world with all
colors in harmony with the other

For my friend *M*
This world is full of colors and you are one of its
Brightest

Home Is

Home is always where the heart is
The soul inside will always be
It is an open heart that fills a courageous soul
Look inside and you'll see that the love around
you is always there
Sometimes it may be a little cloudy, but the home
you built is still there and so sweet

Spilt beans

The daily grind to get us going

It's the frustrating beans spilt in the day that

piss us off

Forget the small stuff and don't sweat it

Stomp the beans and let them be

Spilt beans will never crush the day, it's just a

daily grind and you own the day

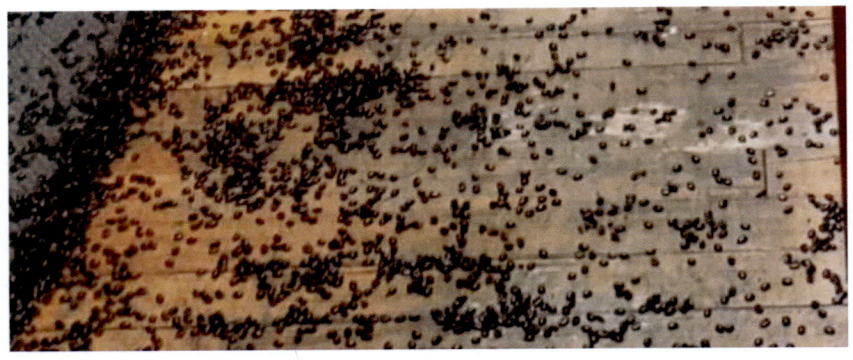

Two Hearts Two Souls

Two hearts beating as one

Two souls living for each other, giving the

freedom to grow independent of the other

We're not perfect alone but perfect for each

other together This is where love grows, as we

nurture the other's needs and desires

Giving our hearts and souls freely to the other;

this is where love is

There's nothing we would change about each

other or who we are, but change together is

where love stays

To have found each other is God's blessing and

taking this journey with you is a chance

we take together

Soul on Fire

It is what grows in our hearts that sets the soul
on fire

It's a feeling that feeds the soul as we embrace
life and who we are

Follow your heart, there is nothing to fear

The soul is on fire, free to explore with passion

Our pursuit of what we have inside of us makes
us fearless

A smile is all it takes to set a soul on fire

A Snowman Melts Away

A snowman melts away and in time will
return again

Though he's gone, his heart and soul

still remains

The snowman will return and live again

Like the snowman I am not lost; I too shall

rise again

It's Your Inner Demon I want

As much as I might have thought it's not your

heart or soul I want

instead I want them to be free to discover and

explore whatever you want

It's your inner Demon I want

She burns hot with every stroke I give

I want only to fill her with a desire for me

whenever she wants, for a moment in time

I want to feel her all over me as you

feel me in you

That's all I want

Sun Sets

Sun sets and another day ends

Like fire in the sky above with vibrant colors

and a beauty within

The power it has will rise again in the morning,

bringing with it a new day

The smile you have shines bright, warming the

heart and filling the soul

A Siren Calls

A Siren calls and my soul awakens
She holds a delicate pearl that guides me
safely to her
As I draw near, the Goddess grants me the
power to capture her with the trident spear that
she set within me
It is her desire and passion that becomes ours
As I see into her soul, it is not I that has
captured her it is she that has captured me
It is this moment in time we are one; together we
are centered in peace with a fire for life that
surrounds us in perfect harmony

Feeling the Rain

A sprinkle upon my head
A soft wind blows and the smell of rain grows
The soul awakens to a fresh and exciting
moment in time

With each new droplet, the music is beating

your song in my heart

The feeling brings a smile and the warmth felt is

in my heart

It feeds the soul, feelings of a

wonderful new start

Soft Silk

Soft silk, light and airy yet strong enough to hold

you up in safety

As you fell, it was the jolt of life you felt, as it

opened up

The rush and excitement of the fall now soft and

slow, with a rejuvenated soul falling ever so

softly with a new outlook in your heart

Would you take a leap of faith in me and

do it again?

A Day in the Snow

I remember a day in the snow with you

It started slow and bumpy yet fun and jumpy

Mid-day it was fast and smooth and a touch of

excitement, with views to remember

At the end we had wet woodies and a bath bomb

for two, to soothe our aching bones

I held you my in arms all night, to wake to

a glorious new day

My only regret is that we didn't find the time to

make a snowman for you

A Deep Blue Sea

A deep blue sea engulfs me

Filled with a beauty that can only be felt and

seen in the heart

Of all there is to discover, there's only one that

ever fed my soul and set my heart on fire, setting

me free of the bonds that had confined me

I found you once and thought that I

had you for a time

We were all that was and nothing came between

us; our thoughts were one, as if we were together

from the very start Only separated by time, the

space was never too great to overcome

As in every journey there are ripples in the

seabed that cause a tidal wave

Lost in a storm I look to the stars to find you

again, so that we may learn to dance once more

The storm may be strong, but no storm is

stronger than the souls and hearts of two friends

that have always been in the heart of the other

Like an angel, you are always in my heart

A Day that Shook my World and Turned it Upside-down

The day I lost sight of who I was is the day

I lost you

I didn't know it then until it was too late

If I could turn back time I

would change me and what I had become

I would not change you

I hadn't realized all I needed to do was just be

me and give you support and something

to laugh about

I can't turn back time or change what happened,

but I can change and begin to heal

With hope, in time that one day we can just say

hello and let the past rest

One day at a time is all we have

Time will take care of the rest

A Dying Soul

A dying soul falls and the heart hardens

The life that was or could have been,

lost in darkness

Both walk alone, cold and lifeless without hope

So too will faith die and fade away, leaving

behind all three

tied together in the burning ashes of what was

Will they rise up again is unknown

Their fate is tied together in search of what will

heal them all, to rise up and soar once more

This is a dying soul

That was originally written about myself while searching for myself to regain what I had lost. Now I have another outlook on what a dying soul is. A dying soul is the memory of what we are. As the last one dies with a memory of ones self the soul will to. I'd like to think that it will live forever in another place and we go on from there.

Destined for a Solitary Life

Destined for a solitary life, this is the nightmare
that keeps me up, frightened to fall asleep
For if I am destined to die alone, who will care
for my four-legged friends who gave me the only
solace I had, as lived this hell on earth, that's my
fear for them
This was not what I wanted, If I had to live it
again, I would not change knowing you, for there
was a time that I wasn't alone
That was and always will be the happiest time
of my life
My greatest fear is if you were to live this life of
solitude also

Transcendent Butterflies

I used to give you butterflies because you used to
give me butterflies
Now we're just an empty cocoon of what was
once beautiful and free
Like life, all things die and come to an end; with
it the amazing memories of what we once had
To let you go was hard, but the hopes and dreams
to fly with you one last time remains
With every passing day, the dream is more
distant and time is no longer on my side
To give you one last flurry of butterflies and set
them free would free my soul and heal my heart
Is it possible to spin one more cocoon and
transcend into flight one more time

I know I will never find another butterfly as
beautiful as you but the amazing smile you left in
me will last forever in my heart.

Feeding Souls

My soul can no longer be captured, only fed

To feed a soul with passion fills the heart

I want to be fed with a passion that fills my

heart and overflows with mine

I want to feed souls with a desire to be fed

No bonds or restraints, as the soul should be

free to explore without limitations

Our souls should not be kept in the corner to

wither away, wanting to be free

Imagine if we all opened our hearts and souls to

feed the Other

Stepping Away

In stepping away, is it really just moving forward? I ask myself this every waning minute of the day. Feeling lost and searching for answers. What I do know is I don't want to lose a friend. I know that I can't imagine a day going by without sharing our thoughts and making her laugh. I know that what's been shared is beyond the usual. I know that what's been shared are things that wouldn't have ever happened between anyone else.

She was Delicate and Fierce

She was delicate like a soft breath of fresh air
One that had me feeling rejuvenated and passionate, yet fierce as a wild fire burning out of control with desire
She was a butterfly floating with beauty, full of grace
Yet soared like an eagle with power and life
Then one day she was gone and the life within me too
Now I must say goodbye and try to find life in me again

A Cold Heart

A cold heart turns to stone and with it the soul

freezes like ice

Locked inside is the beauty that once burned

with passion that had a desire to feed souls

The burning feeling you feel inside your heart is

the passion you have when your heart is open

Its desire to feed the soul will flow like a river or

ocean tide when the heart is free and

open to explore

I believe that one day my passion will thaw and

free the desire to feed once more the

soul I once knew

Open your heart and see what beauty can be

This was not written entirely about anyone person. It was also written about myself and what I became too. I'm searching to find myself again in all the chaos

Pieces of Me

Each piece I write, I give a piece of me
Each piece is for you, from my Heart
If each piece of me falls in your Heart
that's all I could ever want
This piece of me is for you

My Serendipity

My Serendipity
You may have started with a little lust
But what came next was much more than lust
I did not come looking
But one look into your eyes and I saw
something in you
Then I saw you smile and I knew
I found something I wasn't searching for
I just knew by the way I felt
I may have lost you, but you're still
my Serendipity

I hope one day I'll find you again

Good Fortune

To know you is my good fortune

To look into your eyes and see you smile is

enchanting

To hold you in my arms, kiss you and feel your

heartbeat with mine is

living

Sunshine to Vine

From sunshine to vine this rose is meant to share

A day will come when we open a bottle together

and let the sunshine out onto us

We'll savor every drop and share its sweet
gentle kiss on our sultry lips
Nestled up by a fire we'll dance
through the night

Blessings

As you count your blessings, and there are many
You think of the ones you cherish the most
Each different for very special reasons
Each mean so much as you reflect on them
You realize that you are their blessing too
A tear rolls down your cheek
It's not one of sadness, but of joy
As you're overwhelmed by your happiness
Each blessing is filled with love

Our Time

It's our time. Although we've only just begun, our hearts and souls have always known the other. It's our time to come together and start our journey with each other. Together we will conquer the world and live our dreams. It's our time to explore the world together. It's our time.

There's nothing we can't do, now that our hearts and souls have found the other. It's our time. No one or anything can take it away now that we're together. It's our time for friendship, love and all there is for the other. It's our time. Best friends forever, lovers always together. It's our time. You've always known my heart and soul and I've always known yours. It just took a while to find each other. It's our time to move forward together. Never looking back, always knowing that God has brought us together. It's our time now. It's always been our time.

Trust from the Heart and Jump Without Fear

You were scared, and I was there

I could see in your eyes; the spark of light was

still in them, but they didn't sparkle and dance

I felt it in your silence, yet your

silence spoke loudly

I held you letting you know

I'm here with you

Your heart was pounding so hard I could feel it

from ten feet away

We watched others do it while we waited

for our turn

We watched and as a four-legged friend came to

you, your nerves began to calm

Then you spoke a word

The time came to get ready, and every part of

your body was so tense your smile disappeared

Your face was blank for the first time

As we suited up to jump, we made jokes to

calm your nerves

Then I held your hand to let you know

I was there with you

That I know the feeling you had

The walk to the plane, your heart started racing

and your smile returned with excitement

As the plane headed down the strip, your eyes lit

up and started twinkling once again

Up up up, to 13500 feet we went

The door opened and a rush of air came in

You looked at me with a "holy shit this is wild"

One by one you watched others go out the door

Then one final check to make sure

you were safely secure

A scootch to the door and out you went

I followed right behind, watching you

all the way

Feeling and sharing this free fall over the edge

Feeling the exhilarating rejuvenation of life

I wouldn't have shared this with
anyone else but you

The Life I See

I see bright green eyes that are a fresh spring air
to my soul Rejuvenating every breath I take
I see a beautiful smile that is the heart of your
soul and fills mine with a warmth so deep
I see with my heart the life in your eyes that
brings a new life mine
I see with my soul the beautiful smile in you
that is so bright
I see the shinning star that you are
I want to be your shinning star
The life I see in you is the life I want to live
If I could show you the life I see, what a beautiful
smile forever in our hearts will be
The life I see is the life I want with you

Siren in the Sea

There is a Siren in the Sea

I search for my red hair temptress day and night

She is the desires to my fire that burns

within our loins

She has the passion that fills my lust, like a

magnum of wine that keeps our

glasses overflowing

Her treasure there for me, a pearl nestled

between her lips

The kiss she has for me gives a power to me

We devour each other, unleashing all that we

have as I pierce what she gives to me

Let us drink the nectar of the Gods and let it flow

from us as we dance in a sinful bliss

A Picture Tells a Thousand Words and a Tale

A picture will say a thousand words and tell its
tale Sometimes happy, sometimes sad, sometimes
angry, sometimes lost

In it, a glimpse of the soul and a look
into the heart

I once saw a shining light in your eyes in a
picture of you with a vibrant and glowing smile

Now I see a shadow of what was

The twinkle in your eyes is gone and the smile is
no more Just a lost, glazed look and a lost soul
with an empty heart

It saddens me greatly to see and I pray for you

A Fire Inside

She had a fire inside her that burned
like no other

Then one day she sold her soul to another

The fire she had died that day and her smile

was no more

My Heart

Would you have me as I am

I don't have much

What I do have is a big heart filled with all the

love you could want

What I offer is a friendship for life

Always there when you need me

Always there to hold you and dance through life

In good times and in bad

What I give is my heart; my soul will follow, as

the two are always together

They belong to me, but I give them to you

To share our life as we are is all I can ask

right now

I don't wish to change you or to stifle you

Only to one day change your life as you

would want it

I dream of a day where we live on an ocean
beach, walking it each day hand in hand
Would you dream with me now!?
Perhaps one day it will be
Can you see a future where we walk the beach
and dance through life?
If you can, we have more than a chance
We have a bright future that we can
walk together
Would you have me as I am and take a chance
and dream with me now?

Not Perfect

I'm not perfect but neither are you
We all have baggage and that's just fine
Unpack and let it out
It is what it is
I'll accept yours as you accept mine

Nothing to hide

Just let it out

Wine

Sitting here drinking wine

The wine we first shared

Remembering all the amazing times we had

Hoping that someday we can enjoy

each other again

Dreaming of what it could be

I don't know what the future holds

But know if that day comes

I'll hold you in my arms and you'll know

You never left my heart

Halo

My Angel's halo

A golden ring that holds land and sea

Upon its ring, roses cared for by butterflies

that spread life with sweet nectar between

each rose, starfish and seashell

At the center, a single pearl

It is the pure heart of the halo that brings out

the soul in this Angel

Finding You

The day I found you was a beautiful day

It's was a day I'm blessed to have

We talked and became friends

We opened our hearts and found what we had

not set out to find

I found you in my heart and a beautiful new

future began When you wake in the morning and

feel me in your heart you smile and everything

you want is right before you

Your smile is more beautiful than anything

I've ever known

To get you to smile every day for me warms my heart and I see a future so wonderful, as we walk hand in hand on a beach of love and peace we've found in each other

What we set out in search of may not be what we thought we wanted
What we discover may be what we always wanted to begin with
We found each other and that's all we need

Wedges

Wedges that came between us became too much and drove us apart and one us was gone
Always was no more
From the start there was always someone or something that wanted to split us apart
Even after we were split apart there was someone doing more to keep us apart

I pray someday the wedges will no longer be

and we can be free to just be

Deep Pockets Will Never Feed the Soul

Deep pockets won't fill the heart

I have something far greater than deep pockets

It comes from what's inside my heart

I don't need deep pockets to give myself to a

deserving heart The rest falls into place by itself

Deep pockets destroy hopes and dreams with an

emptiness that costs the soul and the heart

The deep pockets that would have you tied up in

bonds in the corner aren't worth your soul and

the heart you have

Dark Canvas

The canvas torn and tattered

The paint dry and tainted

The colors dull and flat

This canvas rancid with no hope

Once vibrant and full of life, this canvas now old

with no soul to feed what once was

Only a dream of a world that does not exist, for

it is an empty heart

This is not how I really feel about the canvas but a reflection of what was lost. How I really feel is what I know will always exist.

Forever In the Stars

Forever in the stars, stories are told and time

stands still

They neither wait for us nor leave us behind

They guide us or tell us of a time long forgotten

Look to them and follow a dream if you will

The dreams you follow fill your soul

Live your dreams and make your stars

Corners

You don't belong in the corner

You are meant to be free and flourish like a

wildflower You're an ocean tide with power that

shapes sand on the beach

To keep you in a corner is to stifle and confine

your true beauty

Still in the corner, confined and restrained

With no space to be who you were meant to be

Take back the beauty of what is still inside and

set yourself free

For you are not meant to be in a corner, with no

soul to be fed

Open your heart and you will see a world of

dreams unfold

Releasing your true beauty

Divine Spark

Every time I see into your eyes, I see a divine

spark that is your soul

I feel it in your heart every time I hold you

in my arms

I feel it in every kiss we share

I feel it in your gentle touch

I hear it in your voice and in your laughter

I see it in your smile

You have a spark that is so empowering, even

when I'm not with you

I close my eyes and imagine I'm with you and

feel your spark

Your love of God, family and friends is the power

of the spark that you are

Natures Song

As I slept so peacefully, dreaming of you

I woke when the storm passed over,

still thinking of you

The sound of the rain is calm and soothing

It's natures love song

I think to myself, dancing with you is what the
song is about

I fall asleep dreaming of us dancing in the rain

Price of an Empty Heart

You once told me what it would take for another
to have your heart

I pray that day never comes, for the price is too
great for you to lose your soul

Your heart is not for sale

Your heart is yours to give, so that it can be
filled by only one

I hope and pray you find the one

The Day We Met

Before we met the days were dark and gray. I felt as if life was going nowhere. I was alone, just going through the motions. That all changed THE day I met you. From the first moment, you challenged me to be a better person and changed my life. Before you, the glass was always half empty. Now the glass is always full with life. That day you opened the door to my heart and touched my soul, lighting a fire deep inside. Every day since that day has been a beautiful new day, filled with sunshine and wondrous colors of life. You put me at ease even when life has brought me down, just by simply listening. Your beautiful smile is one I can't wait to see. Talking with you is always a delightful time, as I know a little more about you each time. I thank God we met and thank God for what's to come. Together the glass flows over with abundant

laughter, joy and a smile that can't be dimmed.
The day we met is an amazing day I'll never
forget.

Free Yourself

Free yourself from those who would have
you in bonds
Free yourself from those who would have
you in a corner
Free yourself from those who would keep
you there
Set yourself free and be who you are meant to be
Wild and free is who you are and who you are
meant to be

Courtesan Scarlet

A brilliant Scarlet Courtesan of the night filled
with a passion for life

Your stunning elegance shall have the desires of those who reach for you

It's your beautiful smile and sparkling eyes that will feed souls

With fierce eyes you captivate the attention of desire for you

The delicate smile you possess releases a passion from deep within
It is the dance between silky rose sheets that rejuvenates and awakens the mind, body and soul

The Monster I Became

I never wanted to become the monster I became
All I ever wanted was to help make things better
In that time, I lost who I was and didn't see what I had become

It wasn't until I lost you that I saw what

I had become

Finding you again will complete finding me and

who I am

Know I never wanted to hurt you

All I ever wanted to do was hold you and be

there for you

Forgive me now, so we can put the past aside

and be who we are meant to be

The monster in me is gone, as I have found

Me again

One Day

One day I'll forgive myself for what I became

All I ever wanted to do was make a difference

In doing so I lost who I was and became a

monster I could not see

Because I did not listen, I lost who and what

was most important in my life

One day I'll forgive myself and pray you will too

One day you'll forgive yourself and know just

how beautiful you truly are

Your heart will open and you'll see what has

always been inside of you

You'll feel what has always been with you...

A Distant Closeness

I feel a distant closeness

Even with the distance between us

There is still a closeness

I feel it in the memory of the things

we once shared

They live in my heart and are a part of my soul

It is that closeness that I will never let go of

or say goodbye to

A Tryst in the Park

A tryst in the park just for two

We'll find our spot with a perfect view

Under a tree we'll pitch a blanket and dig into a

picnic basket

A bottle of wine and some cheese with some

bread, and a nice spread

Some fresh fruits to tickle the palette

With our toes curled in lush green grass

You in my arms and the scent of an ocean breeze

arouses our hearts

Another bottle of wine and the heat of this tryst

will blaze into the sunset and on into the night

under the stars

Enchanting Eyes

Enchanted by your bright green eyes,

my soul is fed as I look into you

Your silky red locks, radiant with a fire of desire

that sets the heart on blaze

It is the passion within your soul that feeds souls,

as they will always be glowing with the soft

touch of heavenly bliss you bring to them

Untitled...to Many

Exquisite vibrant lustrous beauty,

like a breath of fresh spring air

that rejuvenates the soul

One that awakens a heart to your radiance of the

life within you

Gentle Breeze

A gentle sea breeze flowing through soft fiery

red locks

A gaze of tranquil bliss from emerald green eyes

with a twinkle like the night stars

Soft pink lips with a smile that amazes all

A vibrant glow of sunshine surrounds you

like a halo

I think of the phrase

La Vie En Rose

That is the beauty I see in you

Twinkle in Your Eyes

A twinkle in your eyes with a vibrancy that

feeds my desires, my soul to the heart

Its fire and passion within you live and

brighten the day

The sultry smile of seduction is my sunshine

The flowing red locks I see blaze

throughout the day

with a rejuvenation in my breath like fresh air

Pure elegance glows around you and

sparkles in your green eyes

Your beautiful smile with mesmerizing eyes feeds

me and fills my heart

Ems Beach

With fire in your soul that burns in your heart,

the beach you walk will become majestic, as you

bless its golden sand

The sand like silk between your toes, the smile

you bare will be seen

Your beauty is not only on the surface, but deep

within and shines bright day and night

What Makes a Beach

A beach is only sand and water without you

A beach is beautiful when you're on its

golden grains

Its silk sand pillows you as you lay soaking up

sweet sunshine, as your body glows from

the sun's kiss on you

Cool refreshing waves send a mist that's soothing

to the mind, body and soul

As each wave crashes against the shore, it brings

a relaxing and peaceful sound of

music to your ears

That beach is magical when I see

your beautiful smile

To share it with each other is what

makes a beach

Two Hearts

We are two hearts finding our way through life

We thought we had what we wanted

earlier in life

For a time it worked, but wasn't to be

Our hearts were broken and our souls were hurt

We saw something in each other and opened our

hearts again and a friendship began

I see in you a beauty I've never known before

It's in your eyes

I see it in the way that they shine as you

look at me

It's in your smile

So beautiful it is to see as you smile at me

I feel it in your touch with every soft stroke as

you hold my arm as we walk

I feel it in your heart as it beats with mine while

we dance

I hear it in your voice when we talk

I feel like our thoughts are the same

We found each other

Two hearts together as one is a beautiful thing

A Quiet Storm Rages

A quiet storm rages and I know that I'm to blame

Wishing I could turn back time and change the

things I did Wishing I could make right

what was done

Time heals, but trust that's been broken will take

longer and I know that

Missing my best friend, wanting to hold her and

tell her how sorry I am

Hoping this storm passes and that someday

I will be forgiven

You Inspired Me

You inspired me for so long and I was at peace

and knew who I was

I knew who I wanted and what I wanted

Then one day it disappeared and I lost

who I was

Not because I wanted it to

but because I wanted too much

You still inspire me to be a better person and I

can only hope you know how much

you mean to me

Take Your Best Shot

I'm a hack at golf, but that's not what matters

I go out just for the fun of it

Sometimes I do good and have a few pars with a

birdie here and there

Every once in a great while, an attempt at eagle

or a hole in one

Life, like golf, should be just the same

Take your best shot

Swing away and don't hold back

Attack it with fire and passion

Stirred

If I stirred something in you it's because you

stirred something in me

Smile because it's what I did when

I thought of you

What is Love

What is love
Love is many things
Love is caring
Love is kindness
Love is emotions
Love is feelings that come from our souls
Love lives in our hearts
Love will never die, as it is a part of our souls
Love has and always will be in our hearts

Thankful

I've been thinking a lot about this year and feel little to be thankful for. I've made some mistakes I'm so very sorry for. Even though I had the best intentions, I should have left some things alone. All I can do is ask for forgiveness and let time take care of itself. The one thing I'm thankful for is that I know you.

Shadows

Shadows of myself late at night

Thinking of you under the crescent moon

The hopes of dreams within my heart

If only they could be

As We Are

I'll have you as you are

If you'll have me as I am

Just two souls with unbridled passion

for the other

No limits to what can be

Just two open hearts in the moment

This is what life should be

My Shooting Star

I look into the stars at night

Searching for my shooting star to wish upon

When all I had to do

Was look into your sparkling eyes and know that

You're all I needed

Dream of a Beach

Just for two

Walk across golden silk sand

With each grain that passes between the toes

enchanted souls will be felt

As each new wave washes away what was left

behind, the soul is still engrained

With each new wave ahead, it cleanses with a

rejuvenating glance into the sunset

The souls that blessed this beach flow out to sea

Into the night they dance, as the stars glitter

upon each wave

Two will rise to the dawn of a new day

Mystical Northern Lights

Mystical northern lights capture eyes with
brilliant colors and elegance
Your bright green eyes, like the northern lights,
are magical with a vibrant energy that
captures many
It's your smile that lights up another with the
same magical red locks, your halo with a glow
that flows through the soul
That's your true beauty to bring to those who see
you smile

Majestic

Cool silky sands of gold
Crisp refreshing salt air
The oceans rolling waves carve a new path
ashore for us to walk
The power and beauty of this beach becomes
majestic as we embrace

We thank God for all he has given us

Wine Upon Your Sweet Lips

Wine upon your sweet lips like a soft gentle kiss

Your glass reflects your lips and shimmers at me

A look into your eyes and I know it's not the

glistening wine you want on your lips

It's my lips you want

Another sip and we begin to dance and feel life

for what it is

Beach of Dreams

A beach without you is just a place where

ocean meets land

A beach with you becomes a place with golden

sand and sun kissed shoulders

A beach with us is where friendship grows and

possibilities are endless

A beach by itself is a dream waiting to happen

A beach with you awakens and comes to life

A beach with us is magical, as the sun sets the

sounds of the ocean are music to dance to

Tantric Pleasure

This tantric pleasure is a treasure

Where dreams come true

With piercing eyes like a clear blue sky

Her locks that wisp in the wind and a whisper of

a fresh spring air

The scent captures me and feeds my soul

Soft porcelain skin in shear black silk and topped

with sexy lace

I release what's inside of me and explore the

beauty in life with this tantric pleasure

An Unexpected Friend

A time of uncertainty and a time of doubt

An unsuspected friend emerges in the dark

Once a nemesis and a distrusted acquaintance

With an open heart to reach out, extend a hand

and say I'm sorry for your loss

A thank you and a new friend made as the past is

laid to rest

Thank you S

Dolphins in the Cove

Sunrise and dolphins play in the cove

They dance on water to bless this day

We drink mimosas and watch them dance

Their dance is graceful with elegance and finesse

One day we'll dance with them on calm waters

and let the day unfold

Not the same beach

This beach is the same beach

But it's not the same

It's not the same beach, because you're not here

This beach was alive with beauty once

A natural beauty that carried the day

Now it's a faded memory of what it once held

This beach is not the same without you

But I'll keep coming and feel, for just a moment,

that the beauty it once held is still here

Still here, waiting for you

I stand in the waves coming ashore to feel a

rejuvenation waiting to happen

I feel what it once had washing away what was

Not to carry it away, but to let it free and be a

part of the sea

A sea like an open heart, an open heart

like the sea

They are two of the same

Deep and filled with life

Inspire the day

You inspire each day with a beauty that is pure

and natural, and rises with a simplicity

like the sun

You are its sunshine that is felt

You touch and feed the souls of more

than you know

With a smile so pure it brightens even the

gloomiest day

Rising above it all, the fire inside you

burns with life

You are its fresh spring air

The intense gaze in your eyes owns the day

As light gives way to the night, so to will it

belong to you

Time Lost

Time lost or is it lost time

I don't know

I ask myself what was lost

My answer is I still don't know

For whatever it was is lost in time

Is it possible to find the time lost

I don't know

I do know, if I could open the door I would

explore beyond

To find out what may have been lost in time

Only time will tell

Chains of Darkness

Not all chains are of cold steel made to restrain

Some chains are cast in thought and words
meant to restrain the soul

To empty the heart and drain the soul

It's these chains that hurt much more

Cast aside these chains and let your spirit soar

For you are meant to be free and be who you

want to be

Real Thoughts vs Meme

An original thought and a message sent

This is where we should be

It's the open mind able to speak with an

original thought

The closed mind unable to speak or write without

a meaningless meme

A meme that can easily be taken the wrong way

A meme that sends us in opposite directions and

tears us apart

I didn't understand that once and lost everything

I wanted

I despise the meme and what it has done to us

I used a meme once that I thought would

open a discussion

Instead it sent me off into a distant universe

where a piece me died

I should have just spoken my own words and

stayed true to who I am

It was never my intention to send a meme that was insensitive or meant to make someone feel guilty. For that I'm truly sorry if that is what was felt, and I still struggle with it to this day and find it hard to forgive myself

Anger

Anger fueled by jealousy

Not my jealousy

Jealousy of another who could not have what

was once given to me

It is that jealousy that set us apart

Through deceptive lies

You've seen that jealousy in them and told me so
more than once
Open your eyes now and see it again
You'll see me for who I am and who you
once loved
You'll see him for the predator he is

Harvest

Summer comes to an end
Colors change and fruit is juicy, with a kiss
from the sun
The harvest ready to begin
This bounty is something to be shared in time
When the time is right we'll share this
fruitful delight
We'll release the sunshine it has and have
some cheese
But it's the time shared with friends that makes
this bounty a harvest to remember

it is the time we share that

becomes the harvest

Taboo

What is taboo?

What is your taboo?
What is taboo may not be taboo!
I could say my taboo is you? But in reality you're
not taboo to me, only to others that can not
accept us as we are?
Taboo is many things
To the closed mind, taboo is numerous and
daunting to the soul
To the open heart and soul, taboo is
nowhere to be found
In my mind, my heart and my soul
I have no taboo
Only the sweetness of you
To others that see that as taboo, feeds our

lust to explore more

Taboo is described as something, anything, or

anyone being forbidden

So what is taboo for one may not be

taboo for two

Only taboo for a closed mind, unable to see with

an open heart or soul

What Was,

What Is, and the

Unknown

What was, will always be

In what was are the memories of all that

made us who we are

What was, holds treasured times and

lessons learned

With an open mind of what was, what is, is now

the foundation for what is now

The unknown is a future we do not know

So dream and live for today for one day our

dreams may come in ways that are unknown

Still Here

I'm still here for you

Through all that has happened I'm still here

Quit listening to others

Listen to what has always been inside you

I'm still here for you

Ask yourself who believes in you

You'll see I'm still here

For you

Open your heart and look into your soul

You'll know that I never left you

Know that I'm
Thankful

Know that I am thankful to know you

Know that I wish you nothing but happiness

Know how incredible you are and that you are

Beautiful

There is one last dedication who's name shall remain silent, for reasons I can not say of my own. You know who you are, if you are reading this. You know that you are a huge part of this book and what you mean to me. I know that a part of me must let go and that part of me has let go. Another part of me can't let go. It's not in me to give up on you. I will always believe in you, you will always have my love and support in everything you do. You will always be with me in my heart and my soul will always see you for what we had. I know it was real.

Sweet Jolee

Heavenly eyes, I'm lost in the clouds
The sweetest red lips and a smile as beautiful as
a rose
My Jolee feels so soft and silky as we dance in
heavenly bliss
Our hearts beat as one

Ring of Hope

I see your pictures since we last spoke

They give me hope that one day we'll see each

other again They give me hope because I see a

ring that shows you still remember what was

I see the ring and know that always still exists

In my heart I know that one day we'll reunite and

be the friends we always were

I believe in Always, through good times and bad

It's the ring you still bare that gives hope that

Always still remains with you in your heart

As long as you wear the ring I will always

believe in hope and a renewed friendship

Dare To Dream

Dare to dream and reach for your star

Dare to dream and feel what's inside of you

Don't be afraid to share your dreams, they make

you strong and show how beautiful you truly are

Dare to dream and be known for who you are

Dare to dream and explore the unknown, for it's

the spice of life that keeps us new, filled with

hope for a future that is not known

Take your dreams and live, that is the dance

Leave no stone left untouched and

follow your heart

Dare to dream and embrace what you

do not know

Dare to dream and be the spark that ignites a fire

burning with life and passion that feeds souls

My dreams may not be the same as your dreams

but our dreams can dance together in

peace and harmony

Always changing

Always moving forward

Dare to dream, but don't forget the past

For it is who you are and the beauty that grew to

be something wonderful

Not to be forgotten, but remembered

for all time in the heart

Dare to dream

Let your desires burn with an open heart and

flame your passion to dance with another

Dare to dream, but don't dream alone.

I dare to dream, though I don't wish to

dream alone

Will you dream with me for a while and

take a chance

The future is the dreams of everyone around us

in our lives

Dare to dream with me

It's what we do with our dreams that matters

I'm Leaving Now

I'm leaving now

Not to find you, but to find me

Not rebuild what I destroyed and what it is I lost

But to regain my self respect, dignity and honor

within Myself

I have no illusions that you'll be there when I

find Myself

I know you won't, unless some miracle or act of

God falls upon Me

If our paths should cross, then all I could want

is to simply say hello and to know you don't think

ill of me anymore

To Say Goodbye

To say goodbye without having to say goodbye

and dance with you one more time

To know it was all real, to know what was

will always be

To say goodbye and set myself free

To say goodbye my friend

I wish you well